BASEBALL LEGENDS

Hank Aaron
Grover Cleveland Alexander
Ernie Banks
Johnny Bench
Yogi Berra
Roy Campanella
Roberto Clemente
Ty Cobb
Dizzy Dean
Joe DiMaggio
Bob Feller
Jimmie Foxx
Lou Gehrig
Bob Gibson
Rogers Hornsby
Walter Johnson
Sandy Koufax
Mickey Mantle
Christy Mathewson
Willie Mays
Stan Musial
Satchel Paige
Brooks Robinson
Frank Robinson
Jackie Robinson
Babe Ruth
Tom Seaver
Duke Snider
Warren Spahn
Willie Stargell
Honus Wagner
Ted Williams
Carl Yastrzemski
Cy Young

CHELSEA HOUSE PUBLISHERS

TED WILLIAMS

Rick Wolff

Introduction by
Jim Murray

Senior Consultant
Earl Weaver

CHELSEA HOUSE PUBLISHERS
New York • Philadelphia

Published by arrangement with
Chelsea House Publishers.
Newfield Publications is a federally
registered trademark of Newfield
Publications, Inc.

CHELSEA HOUSE PUBLISHERS

Editor-in-Chief: Richard S. Papale
Executive Managing Editor: Karyn Gullen Browne
Copy Chief: Philip Koslow
Picture Editor: Adrian G. Allen
Art Director: Nora Wertz
Manufacturing Director: Gerald Levine
Systems Manager: Lindsey Ottman
Production Coordinator: Marie Claire Cebrián-Ume

Baseball Legends
Senior Editor: Richard Rennert

Staff for TED WILLIAMS
Designer: Diana Blume
Picture Researcher: Alan Gottlieb
Cover Illustration: Daniel O'Leary
Editorial Assistant: Laura Petermann

Library of Congress Cataloging-in-Publication Data
Wolff, Rick, 1951–
Ted Williams/Rick Wolff; introduction by Jim Murray.
p. cm.
Includes bibliographical references (p.   ) and index.
Summary: A biography of the outstanding Boston Red Sox slugger.
ISBN 0-7910-1194-1
0-7910-1228-X (pbk.)
1. Williams, Ted, 1918——Juvenile literature.   2. Baseball players—United
States—Biography—Juvenile literature.   3. Boston Red Sox (Baseball
team)—History—Juvenile literature.   [1. Williams, Ted, 1918–
2. Baseball players.]   I. Title.
GV865.W5W65   1992   91-28438
796.357'092—dc20   CIP
[B]   AC

CONTENTS

WHAT MAKES A STAR 6
Jim Murray

CHAPTER 1
.406 9

CHAPTER 2
THE SLUGGER FROM SAN DIEGO 15

CHAPTER 3
THE KID 19

CHAPTER 4
GREAT EXPECTATIONS 23

CHAPTER 5
ON THE ATTACK 31

CHAPTER 6
THE SPLENDID SPLINTER 39

CHAPTER 7
AT WAR AGAIN 45

CHAPTER 8
"THE GREATEST
HITTER WHO EVER LIVED" 53

CHRONOLOGY 59
STATISTICS 61
FURTHER READING 62
INDEX 63

WHAT MAKES A STAR

Jim Murray

No one has ever been able to explain to me the mysterious alchemy that makes one man a .350 hitter and another player, more or less identical in physical makeup, hard put to hit .200. You look at an Al Kaline, who played with the Detroit Tigers from 1953 to 1974. He was pale, stringy, almost poetic-looking. He always seemed to be struggling against a bad case of mononucleosis. But with a bat in his hands, he was King Kong. During his career, he hit 399 home runs, rapped out 3,007 hits, and compiled a .297 batting average.

Form isn't the reason. The first time anybody saw Roberto Clemente step into the batter's box for the Pittsburgh Pirates, the best guess was that Clemente would be back in Double A ball in a week. He had one foot in the bucket and held his bat at an awkward angle—he looked as though he couldn't hit an outside pitch. A lot of other ballplayers may have had a better-looking stance. Yet they never led the National League in hitting in four different years, the way Clemente did.

Not every ballplayer is born with the ability to hit a curveball. Nor is exceptional hand-eye coordination the key to heavy hitting. Big-league locker rooms are filled with players who have all the attributes, save one: discipline. Every baseball man can tell you a story about a pitcher who throws a ball faster than anyone has ever seen but who has no control on or *off* the field.

The Hall of Fame is full of people who transformed themselves into great ballplayers by working at the sport, by studying the game, and making sacrifices. They're overachievers—and winners. If you want to find them, just watch the World Series. Or simply read about New York Yankee great Lou Gehrig; Ted Williams, "the Splendid Splinter" of the Boston Red Sox; or the Dodgers' strikeout king Sandy Koufax.

A pitcher *should* be able to win a lot of ballgames with a 98-miles-per-hour fastball. But what about the pitcher who wins 20 games a year with a fastball so slow that you can catch it with your teeth? Bob Feller of the Cleveland Indians got into the Hall of Fame with a blazing fastball that glowed in the dark. National League star Grover Cleveland Alexander got there with a pitch that took considerably longer to reach the plate; but when it did arrive, the pitch was exactly where Alexander wanted it to be—and the last place the batter expected it to be.

There are probably more players with exceptional ability who didn't make it to the major leagues than there are who did. A number of great hitters, bored with fielding practice, had to be dropped from their team because their home-run production didn't make up for their lapses in the field. And then there are players like Brooks Robinson of the Baltimore Orioles, who made himself into a human vacuum cleaner at third base because he knew that working hard to become an expert fielder would win him a job in the big leagues.

A star is not something that flashes through the sky. That's a comet. Or a meteor. A star is something you can steer ships by. It stays in place and gives off a steady glow; it is fixed, permanent. A star works at being a star.

And that's how you tell a star in baseball. He shows up night after night and takes pride in how brightly he shines. He's Willie Mays running so hard his hat keeps falling off; Ty Cobb sliding to stretch a single into a double; Lou Gehrig, after being fooled in his first two at-bats, belting the next pitch off the light tower because he's taken the time to study the pitcher. Stars never take themselves for granted. That's why they're stars.

1

.406

O n September 28, the last day of the 1941 baseball season, Ted Williams, the 23-year-old left fielder for the Boston Red Sox, spent the morning wandering the nearly deserted streets of Philadelphia with his friend Johnny Orlando, the team's clubhouse man. Several times the two men entered a drugstore to get a serving of ice cream. But mostly they just walked.

Williams was nervous, as nervous as Orlando had ever seen him. Who could blame him? That afternoon, in a doubleheader at Shibe Park against the Philadelphia Athletics, his whole season was going to be on the line.

Boston's pennant hopes had ended nearly a month earlier, when the New York Yankees had clinched the American League championship. Williams, however, was still in a white-hot race. It had nothing to do with teams or pennants but with hitting .400 for the season.

A magical batting average, .400 placed a hitter up there with Ty Cobb and Rogers Hornsby and Shoeless Joe Jackson. Not since 1923, when Harry Heilmann of the Detroit

The hard-hitting Ted Williams in 1941, his third year as a major leaguer and a season when his mighty bat ripped the American League apart.

Tigers hit .403, had anybody in the American League batted .400 for a season. Not for a decade, not since Bill Terry of the New York Giants hit .401 in 1930, had anybody in the National League done it.

Even though he was in just his third big league season, Williams knew that he belonged with the game's greatest hitters. He wanted to hit .400 more than anything in the world, he told Orlando as they walked down one unfamiliar street after the other. He would be shattered—"the most disappointed guy in the world"—if he did not make it.

Williams had hit over .400 virtually all year. His average slipped below the magical percentage only for 3 weeks in May and 13 days in July. But now, on the last day of the season, his average was hanging by a thread.

Williams was tired, and it showed. The day before, he had managed only one hit in four trips to the plate, and his average had dropped from .401 to .3995. Rounded off to the third decimal, which was how baseball statisticians figured batting averages, his mark stood exactly at .400.

Williams could cash in his chips and settle for the rounded-off average. Joe Cronin, the Red Sox manager, urged the young star to take the day off. By not playing Sunday, his average would be preserved. If he played both games of the Sunday doubleheader and, as might be expected, came to bat eight times, he would need at least four hits to stay above .400.

"I figure a man's a .400 hitter, or he isn't," Williams said. No matter what the statisticians said, .3995 was not .400. He would play.

On the mound for Philadelphia in the first game was Dick Fowler, a newcomer from the

Boston Red Sox manager Joe Cronin (right) discusses the finer points of hitting with Williams at Boston's Fenway Park in 1941.

Athletics' Toronto farm team. With the pennant race settled early, the American League clubs had called up a number of their minor league players. And Williams was convinced that facing unfamiliar pitchers had hurt his pursuit of .400. "I was going along as smooth as you please," he said later, "and suddenly in the last month my average tailed off. . . . The main reason was that I was swinging against a lot of birds up for late-season tryouts."

Williams needed to know how a pitcher threw and how he thought. "You can't outsmart the pitch," Williams liked to say, "but you can outsmart the pitcher." And he could not outsmart a pitcher he did not know.

But on this September afternoon, he did not have to outsmart Dick Fowler. Seventy-nine-year-old Connie Mack, in his 41st year as owner and manager of the Athletics, had given his pitchers clear instructions: Get Williams out, but throw him strikes. The old sportsman wanted no part of intentional walks or high, inside, unhittable pitches.

Fowler's first two pitches to Williams were balls. From the Philadelphia dugout, Mack glared at the pitcher. Fowler got the message and delivered his next pitch across the plate.

Trying to get Williams out by throwing him a strike was like trying to calm a shark by throwing it a steak. Williams lived for strikes. With eyesight so sharp that some people claimed he could read the label on a record as it whirled rapidly on a turntable, Williams could see a strike coming almost as soon as the pitcher released the ball. Then, at the last split second, he would swing. Long, smooth, endlessly practiced, his swing gained power from a precise pivot of the hips and drew its precision from a little snap of the elbow.

Williams's swing was beautiful, and it was mighty. Not only was his batting average at .400 coming into the doubleheader, but he had smashed 36 home runs to lead the league. Meanwhile, he had struck out only 27 times.

When Fowler's third pitch came zooming across the plate, Williams tagged it past first base and into right field. In the fourth inning, he displayed his power by crashing the ball over the center-field wall. In the sixth, he singled to left field. In the seventh, he singled again. An inning later, he reached base on an error.

With everything on the line, Williams had gone four for five. His batting average had jumped to .404. Even if he went hitless in the second game, his average would not dip below

.400. Playing loose, with his teammates cheering him every time he stepped to the plate, Williams notched two more hits in the nightcap to lift his batting average to .406.

In the years that followed, Williams, never a prisoner of false modesty, liked to ask his teammates around the batting cage before games, "Am I the greatest hitter of all time?" Although they had long since tired of the question, they never hesitated with the answer: "Sure, Ted." And, to a man, they meant it.

2

THE SLUGGER FROM SAN DIEGO

Theodore Samuel Williams was born on August 30, 1918, in San Diego, California, a little city with a nearly perfect climate. When Ted was a boy, his parents, Sam and May Williams, tended quite often to be away from home trying to find work. To fill in the hours, Ted played sports with the neighborhood kids. But even though he had a younger brother, Danny, Ted spent much of the time by himself. Early on, people began to speak of him as a loner.

His mother, who was involved in the Salvation Army and other church-related activities, had a strong influence on Ted's early years— including his choice of sports. When Ted was only six, he loved to play tennis. But when the expensive strings of his racquet began to break, his mother pushed him to play baseball in the hope that the sport would prove less costly.

As the young Ted Williams grew, it became apparent that his mother had the right idea when she handed him a bat and ball. Ted himself knew that he could play well, but he was not

The future Hall of Famer (left) at age six, with his mother, May, and brother, Danny.

Williams attracted the attention of several major league scouts once he began starring on the Herbert Hoover High School baseball team in San Diego, California. The Boston Red Sox finally signed him in June 1936, only a few days after he graduated.

certain just how well. He worried about making his high school team. So when he heard that a new high school was opening, he pleaded with his mother to send him there. Being brand new, Herbert Hoover High School would have a smaller enrollment than his old school, and so it would be easier for him to make the baseball team.

Ted not only made the team at Hoover, but he quickly established himself as a terrific high school player. He was so good, in fact, that baseball scouts were soon coming by to watch him.

One of the first people to spot Ted's potential was connected to a semipro ballclub sponsored by a company that distributed liquor. Ted was thrilled by the offer to be paid to play the game he loved. But his mother, still involved in church-related activities, said no to the deal.

There were soon other opportunities for Ted. The St. Louis Cardinals invited him to a local tryout camp. Ted had gotten hurt a few days before the tryout, however, and did not play well. The Cardinals failed to offer him a contract.

Nevertheless, word of Ted's hitting prowess continued to spread. One afternoon, while playing in a high school game, he belted a tremendous home run that not only cleared the outfield but kept going until it crashed into a store window. Bill Essick, a scout for the New York Yankees, saw the shot. Hoping that he could get the Yankees the inside track, Essick went to Ted's home to talk about the gigantic home run. But when the scout got there, Ted's mother answered the doorbell.

By now, May Williams had heard about the shattered store window from her son. Fearing that replacing the window would be costly, she was a bit nervous when an unknown man appeared at her door.

"Are you Mrs. Williams?" Essick asked as the door opened.

"Yes, I am," she said. "And I imagine you're here about the broken window, correct?"

"Yes, ma'am, I sure am!"

At that point, Ted's mother practically shut the door in Essick's face. Indeed, it took several minutes for the scout to clear up the confusion about the broken window and to let her know that he was there to congratulate young Ted, not to punish him.

But it was not the Yankees who signed him. At the tender age of 17, fresh out of Hoover High School, the 6-foot-3-inch, 160-pound Williams signed with the Boston Red Sox. And to top it off, he did not have far to travel to begin his career. The Boston front office assigned the young man to the Red Sox farm team in San Diego.

3

THE KID

In June 1936, Ted Williams began playing for the San Diego Padres of the Pacific Coast League. He was paid $150 a month, a handsome salary for an 18-year-old in the middle of the Great Depression.

As a rookie outfielder, Williams hardly set the baseball world on fire. In his first professional at-bat, against a solid pitcher named Cotton Pippen, the young Williams, batting left-handed, promptly struck out on three pitches.

Williams spent a total of three years in the minor leagues. He never hit over .300 in either of his two years with San Diego, but it was apparent to most observers that as he matured, he would definitely become a threat at the plate. He had tremendous wrist strength and the eyes of a hawk. With his power and patience, he appeared to have a great future.

Like so many great players, Williams did have one major flaw in his game. It was not a physical flaw. Rather, he had a problem with keeping his emotions in check.

In 1938, Williams was invited to spring training with the Red Sox in Sarasota, Florida.

Williams was 17 years old when he began his professional baseball career by playing for the San Diego Padres of the Pacific Coast League.

19

The 6-foot-3-inch Williams (center) during spring training in 1938, shortly before the Boston Red Sox sent the rangy outfielder to their International League ballclub for some more seasoning.

Although his talent impressed the Boston front office, they decided that the 19-year-old was still a bit too young and raw for the big leagues. Williams was told that he was going to play the 1938 season with Boston's top minor league team, the Minneapolis Millers of the International League.

Most young men would have viewed this move as a step up to a higher classification of professional ball. Williams did not see it that way. With a strong, even overpowering, self-confidence, he announced that the Red Sox were obviously making a mistake, that not only was he more talented right now than their three starting outfielders, but that someday he would make more money than all three of them combined.

The Boston sportswriters found Williams's claim to be a delicious story. It was not long before he had built a reputation as something of a loudmouth.

Williams dutifully reported to Minneapolis and had a terrific year. He ended up leading the league in hitting, home runs, and runs batted in. But perhaps because of his cocky attitude and his quick anger—once, back in the dugout after having popped up with the bases loaded, he smashed a water cooler with his fist, almost severing some tendons in his hand—he was not awarded the International League's Most Valuable Player Award; it was shared by two other players.

Still, the season did have its share of bright personal moments. For starters, Williams got to work with Rogers Hornsby, who was serving as a coach with the Minneapolis ballclub. In 1924, playing for the St. Louis Cardinals, Hornsby had posted the all-time highest batting average for a season, .424. He had retired from baseball with a career average of .358, second only to Ty Cobb's .367.

Just as important, Williams met and fell in love with a young woman named Doris Soule. Wedded in 1944, they had one daughter, Barbara Joyce. (Ted was to be married twice more, to Lee Howard and to Dolores Wettach, with whom he had two children, John Henry and Claudia.)

When the 1939 season ended, Williams was clearly on his way to the big leagues. The Red Sox, however, already boasted three of the best outfielders in the majors: Ben Chapman, Doc Cramer, and Joe Vosmik. There appeared to be no room in the team's outfield for the brash, outspoken lefty from San Diego whom some people were already calling the Kid.

4

GREAT EXPECTATIONS

In December 1938, the Boston Red Sox made room for Ted Williams by trading right fielder Ben Chapman to the Cleveland Indians. At the time, the Boston fans and press were skeptical. After all, Chapman was a solid player, having hit .340 in 1938 and over .300 lifetime. Why give him up to make room for a rookie, a brash and loudmouthed rookie at that?

As the 1939 season approached, Williams heard the complaints of the Red Sox fans and quickly dismissed their fears. He had some ups and downs during spring training. In one exhibition game, he got so angry at himself for a poor performance at the plate that he threw a ball over the outfield fence. But there were far more bright moments. One afternoon, he thrilled the fans and amazed his teammates by walloping a massive home run over a distant fence that only a shot off the bat of Babe Ruth had cleared.

When the 1939 season started on April 20, with a game in New York against the Yankees, Williams, batting sixth in the order, struck out in his first two plate appearances. In his third at-bat, he slashed a line drive double off the wall

Williams wore a Boston Red Sox uniform for 19 seasons and played all his home games at Fenway Park. Even though the stadium's right field was one of the deepest in the American League, making it a desert of lost hopes for power-hitting left-handed batters such as Williams, he averaged 27 homers a year.

in right-center field. He showed the fans that he could field, too. His first chance in the big leagues came when he speared a line drive off the bat of Lou Gehrig.

It was a bittersweet moment. Not only was it Williams's first big league performance; but within two weeks, the deathly sick Gehrig, after playing in 2,130 consecutive games, would have to excuse himself from the starting lineup.

Three days later, on April 23, Williams debuted in the place that would be his baseball home for the next 22 years: Fenway Park, a stadium that the writer John Updike has called "a lyric little bandbox of a ballpark." Nothing about Fenway was regular or symmetrical. The high left-field wall, painted bright green and known as the Monster, stood only 315 feet from home plate; it was almost close enough for a hitter,

An outspoken Williams conducts a clubhouse interview with members of the Boston sporting press. Never one to keep his opinions to himself, the American League slugger often made comments that stirred up the local reporters.

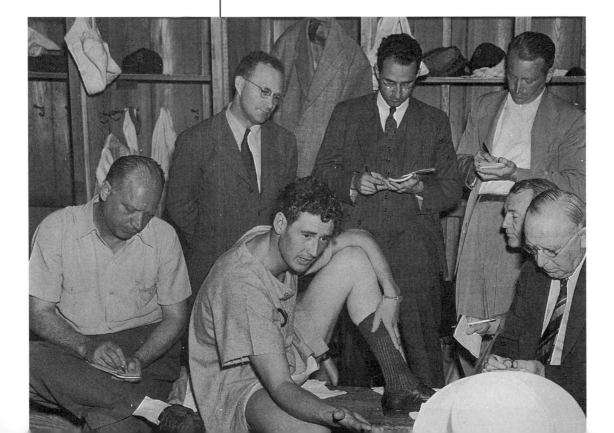

especially a right-handed batter, to reach with a pop fly. The park's right field, however, was one of the deepest in the American League; it was a desert of lost hopes for power-hitting left-handed batters such as Williams. Throughout his career, Williams generally pulled the ball to right field, which meant that he rarely took advantage of the short left-field fence.

In his home debut, Williams electrified Boston with a four-for-five day, including a double and a home run. Oddly enough, two of his hits were off Cotton Pippen, who had struck out Williams on three pitches in his first pro at-bat.

Throughout the rest of the 1939 season, Williams continued to pound the baseball. He finished the year hitting .327 and clubbing 31 home runs, falling just four round-trippers shy of Jimmie Foxx for the American League lead. Williams's 44 doubles were the second most in the league, and he also finished second in runs scored, with 131, and in bases on balls, with 107. He paced the circuit in total bases, with 344. And he led the American League in runs batted in with 145, the most ever by a rookie.

"When I walk down the street," Williams said earlier that year, "I want people to say, 'There goes the greatest hitter who ever lived.'" By the end of 1939, he had taken the first major step toward that goal.

The spring of 1940 brought great expectations for Williams, but things turned sour with the Boston sporting press. His relationship with the local sportswriters had been fine during his sensational rookie year. But now, in his second season in Fenway, he found that the reporters demanded more of him. As they did so, Williams

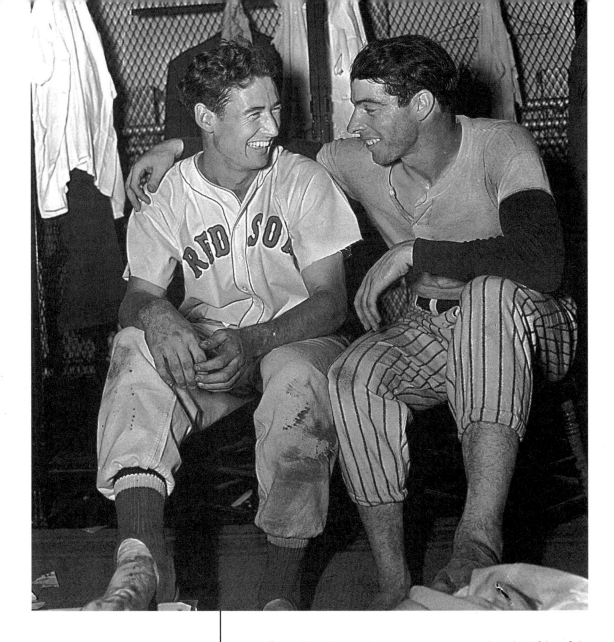

Baseball's two biggest stars in 1941, Williams and New York Yankees center fielder Joe DiMaggio (right), share a laugh moments after the Red Sox outfielder's three-run homer won the 1941 All-Star Game in the bottom of the ninth inning.

refused to keep his emotions in check. If he felt someone had written something unfair or unkind, he would simply blurt out all sorts of criticisms to the press—and many of these outbursts came back to haunt him.

On the ballfield, the 1940 season was another fine one for Williams. He finished the year batting .344. But his home run total dropped to 23 from 31. The Boston sportswriters picked on him for his drop in home run production, particularly because the fences in Fenway had been shortened before the season to help him slug more home runs.

Some of the criticism was downright funny. After one poor performance, Williams said to the reporters in a fit of anger that he should not be a baseball player anymore: "I oughta be a fireman instead." Sure enough, the story made big headlines in Boston. And the next day, when the Red Sox faced the White Sox, the Chicago players were ready for Williams. When he stepped to the plate, the entire White Sox dugout erupted with fire bells, and the players wore firemen's helmets to honor Ted's career wishes.

There were also outbursts that were not so funny. In August 1940, Williams shocked his fans and the Boston reporters by exclaiming that he wanted to be traded, that he had had enough of Boston, and that he was underpaid. His comments did nothing to help his image with the Boston fans. Even worse, the press, instead of letting up on Williams, tried to stir up more controversy.

In 1941, Williams managed to quiet the press by having one of the greatest baseball seasons of all time. His year began slowly. He had injured his ankle in spring training and was limited to pinch-hitting duties during the first two weeks of the season. But by late April, he was back in the lineup and battering American League pitchers at a ferocious clip.

Not only was 1941 the glorious year that Williams hit .406, boasted a league-best .735 slugging percentage, led the league in homers with 37, and drove in 120 runs; it was also the year that Joe DiMaggio of the New York Yankees collected at least one base hit in 56 consecutive games. Believing that hitting a baseball, day in and day out, is the most demanding thing in all of sports, Williams was in awe of DiMaggio's streak.

So was the nation. A history class in Cincinnati voted the Yankees center fielder the most important American of all time, well ahead of George Washington and Abraham Lincoln. A jaunty song about his exploits, "Joltin' Joe DiMaggio," became a popular hit. People everywhere praised DiMaggio's polished manners and angular good looks.

The 1941 season established Williams and DiMaggio as the two premier players in the game, and this led to many comparisons. Williams seldom got the best of it. Both were shy men, uncomfortable with all the attention, but DiMaggio hid his shyness amid a dignified air of privacy. He seldom showed any emotion on the field and never berated sportswriters. Williams did precisely the opposite. What the public often saw was a courtly DiMaggio and a hot-tempered Williams.

In an open letter to the Boston slugger, sportswriter Jimmy Cannon hit where it hurt. "You would take a ball an inch out of the strike zone even if the game was on the bases," he said to Williams. "DiMaggio would hit the bad pitch if he had a chance to drive in an important run."

At the end of the 1941 season, the nation's baseball writers, no friends of Williams's, voted to give DiMaggio the American League's Most Valuable Player Award.

Still, 1941 was a golden year. During the All-Star Game that season, with the American

League trailing 5–4 with two out in the bottom of the ninth inning, Williams came through with a clutch three-run homer that won the game. Williams loved that moment and often referred to it as one of his most thrilling in baseball.

5
ON
THE ATTACK

On December 7, 1941, Japanese forces attacked and bombed Pearl Harbor, a U.S. naval base in Hawaii. The next day, President Franklin D. Roosevelt requested and received from Congress a declaration of war. Young, able-bodied men were then eligible to be drafted into the armed forces. Some of those millions of men were famous ballplayers, Ted Williams among them.

In 1942, Williams was classified by his draft board as being unlikely to be drafted. His exemption came because his mother was solely dependent upon him for support. (His mother and father had divorced some years earlier.) But soon his draft board reconsidered Williams's situation and reclassified him so that he could be called up by the army at any time.

Williams did not agree with this reclassification and appealed the ruling. A short time later, he was given back his previous classification. Unfortunately for him, the press picked up on the story and decided to paint a very unflattering picture of Williams as somebody who did not want to fight for his country.

Naval air cadet Williams gazes at his fiancée, Doris Soule, who in 1944 became his wife. All told, he was married three times and had three children.

31

A glum-looking Lieutenant Williams (center) at Florida's Pensacola Naval Base, where he was stationed for much of World War II. Serving in the military caused him to miss three major league seasons during his prime as an athlete.

Despite the uncertainty about his draft status, Williams put together one of his finest seasons in 1942. He batted .356, hit 36 home runs, drove in 137 runs, and thus won the coveted Triple Crown. But the fans, even those in Fenway Park, did not seem to appreciate him. He was frequently booed and taunted.

Sometimes the fans got to Williams. During a game at Fenway in July, he loafed on the bases and spent his time between innings directing hostile gestures at spectators. Manager Joe Cronin benched and fined him for the episode.

Back in the lineup the next day, Williams apologized for his behavior. But he was less than sorry. He said, in speaking of his tormentors in the stands, "Some day I'm going to take about 25 pounds of hamburger out there and invite those wolves to come down and enjoy it. . . . Then I thought I'd drive some fouls into the left-field stand and knock some teeth out."

At least Williams's critics could no longer shout, "Draft dodger." During the 1942 season, he signed up for the aviation program of the U.S. Navy, and in November he officially went on duty as a naval cadet. He passed the exams necessary to become a pilot but did not see combat. Instead, he became a flight instructor.

In late 1943, Williams was assigned to the naval base in Pensacola, Florida. He spent most of the war years there, helping in the training of pilots and playing baseball at the base. While at Pensacola, he also took up the sport of fishing. It soon turned into one of his major passions, and he became as good at it as he was at hitting a baseball.

During Williams's stint in the navy, his eyesight was tested and officially listed as being

20/10, which meant that he could see far better than a person with normal vision could. The Navy was deeply impressed by Williams's remarkable eyesight, but the discovery was hardly news to American League pitchers, who got another look at him in the spring of 1946, the year after World War II came to an end.

The Red Sox slugger picked up where he left off. He enjoyed a great season in 1946, hitting .342 with 38 homers and 123 runs batted in. He also led Boston to the American League pennant.

During the 1946 All-Star Game, played at Boston's Fenway Park, Williams was once more the star. He connected for two home runs, the second one coming off Rip Sewell's Eephus Pitch, which slowly looped high in the air before coming across the plate. Williams waited and waited, then timed his swing perfectly and drilled the pitch into the right-center-field grandstand.

Batting in front of his hometown fans at the 1946 All-Star Game, Williams clouts Rip Sewell's high-arcing Eephus Pitch for the second of his two home runs that afternoon.

At Fenway Park on July 14, 1946, the left-handed-hitting Williams (at the plate) faces the Boudreau Shift for the first time ever. Devised by Cleveland Indians manager Lou Boudreau to stop Williams from pulling the ball to right field, this defensive alignment employed three infielders on the right side of the diamond, leaving only the third baseman on the left side of the infield.

When the regular season resumed after the All-Star break, Cleveland Indians manager Lou Boudreau employed a new defense against Williams. On July 14, the manager introduced the Boudreau Shift, a defensive alignment specifically designed to stop the Boston slugger, a left-handed hitter who loved to pull every pitch to right field.

After Williams knocked in eight runs in the first game of a doubleheader against Cleveland,

Boudreau knew he had to do something in the
second game to quiet the all-star's bat. When
Williams came up to the plate, the manager
positioned his shortstop behind second base
and asked the Indians first baseman and second
baseman to play far to the right side of the diamond. Such a shift left only the third baseman
to guard the entire left side of the infield.
Boudreau also directed his outfielders to shade
way over to the right side of the field.

Boudreau was trying to tempt Williams to give up pulling the ball and instead take an easy single by hitting the ball to the left side of the diamond. The Cleveland skipper figured that he would rather give Williams a base hit to left than risk his hitting a homer to right.

For the most part, the shift worked well. Williams refused to alter his approach to hitting. "I'm not going to tamper with my style just to hit a few extra singles to left," he said. "I've spent too many years learning how to pull the ball to right to take chances."

The shift backfired one time, however, in a game late in the season, when the Red Sox were playing the Indians and hoping to clinch the American League pennant. Williams came to the plate in the middle of a scoreless game. Sure enough, Boudreau called for the shift. But this time, Williams popped a ball to the left side of the field. By the time the chunky Cleveland left fielder, "Fat Pat" Seerey, had retrieved the ball from the left-field corner, Williams had circled the bases for a home run—the only run of the game—and with the Boston victory came the American League pennant. For Williams, who hit 521 career round-trippers, it was his only inside-the-park home run.

In the National League, the Brooklyn Dodgers and the St. Louis Cardinals finished the 1946 season tied for first. As a result, they held a one-game playoff to determine the pennant winner. In the meantime, to stay sharp, the Red Sox played an exhibition game against a group of American League all-stars. During the contest, Williams was hit on the elbow by a pitch thrown by Mickey Haffner. The injury proved to be so severe that it affected Williams's performance in the World Series.

When the 1946 Fall Classic got underway, Boston was a heavy favorite against the National League playoff champs, St. Louis. But Williams could only manage a disappointing 5 for 25 at the plate because of his sore elbow, and the Cardinals upset the Red Sox, four games to three. Boston would get close to the American League pennant in the remaining years that Williams played for the team, but he never again reached the World Series.

6

THE SPLENDID SPLINTER

Around Fenway Park, Ted Williams maintained his running public feud with the Boston sportswriters. Meanwhile, he was performing good deeds off the field that rarely were reported in the sports pages. For example, after receiving his share of the 1946 World Series money, he quietly donated his money to the Boston Red Sox clubhouse man, Johnny Orlando. In addition, he became involved in raising money for the Jimmy Fund, a Boston-based charity that researches cures for cancer.

These actions may not have made headlines, but Williams's play on the ballfield sure did. In 1947, the Splendid Splinter, as he was sometimes called, captured the second Triple Crown of his career, hitting .343 with 32 home runs and 114 runs batted in. The season was a frustrating one for Williams, however, because the Boston Red Sox finished a poor third in the American League.

Throughout the 1947 season, more and more ballclubs used the Boudreau Shift against Williams. Rather than slap a few singles to left

A perfectionist as a ball-player, Williams traveled regularly to Kentucky to supervise the making of his Louisville Slugger bats by Hillerich and Bradsby.

Perhaps the most selective hitter of all time, Williams virtually never swung at a bad pitch. He rarely struck out and trailed only Babe Ruth in the category of most walks drawn in a career. "He waited so long," Hall of Fame catcher Bill Dickey said of Williams, "that I swear I caught some of the balls he hit."

field, he still insisted on pulling the ball to right. At one point, his batting average dropped to around the .270 mark, and the Boston press begged him to be more of a team player and to hit more balls to left field. Williams refused, and the reporters made his life unbearable.

Before long, the Boston slugger was more convinced than ever that the sportswriters were out to get him. When they voted for the American League's most valuable player for the 1947 season, they overlooked his second Triple Crown performance and handed the award to Joe DiMaggio. The New York Yankees star beat out Williams for the honor by the slimmest of margins, one point. It turned out that one of the Boston sportswriters, Mel Webb, who disliked Williams, had left the Red Sox star entirely off his ballot! Even a 10th-place vote by Webb would have enabled Williams to win the award.

As frustrating as 1947 was, 1948 and 1949 were worse. Both years saw the Red Sox battle to the wire, only to lose the pennant on the last day of the season. In 1948, Boston ended the regular season tied for first place with the Cleveland Indians. The Red Sox lost the playoff game between the two teams, 8–3. Then, in 1949, Boston held a one-game lead with two games left against the second-place Yankees. All the Red Sox had to do to capture the pennant was win one of the two games.

New York took the first game, 5–4, to move into a tie with Boston. Nearly 70,000 fans packed Yankee Stadium to see the showdown. The home team nursed a 1–0 lead into the eighth inning and then scored four runs off Red Sox left-hander Mel Parnell. Once again, Boston had just missed a trip to the World Series.

Williams did his part both seasons. In 1948, he batted .369, his highest average since 1941. And in 1949, while leading all hitters in the league in walks for the sixth straight year, he came within an eyelash of his third Triple Crown. He won a fourth RBI title and fourth home run championship, missing out only on the batting title.

The chase for the 1949 American League batting championship, like the pennant race, went down to the last few days. On September 29, Williams was leading the league with an average of .346; the Detroit Tigers' George Kell trailed him with .342. Then Williams went into a slump. Over the final four games, he went 1 for 11. And when Kell went 2 for 3 on the final day of the season, he ended up nipping Williams for the batting crown, finishing at .3429 and to Williams's .3427. As a result, the Boston outfielder missed the Triple Crown by two ten-thousandths of a point.

A dejected Williams is surrounded by jubilant New York fans as the Yankees tie the Boston Red Sox for first place heading into the final day of the 1949 American League season. The following afternoon, for the second year in a row, the Red Sox lost the pennant by dropping the regular season's last game.

*A sliding Williams tries
unsuccessfully to avoid a
tag by New York Yankees
catcher Yogi Berra in the
heat of the 1951 pennant
race.*

The following year saw Williams suffer more personal setbacks. He started the 1950 season with greater determination than ever to see the Red Sox reach the World Series, but he fractured his arm near the elbow in the All-Star Game while trying to catch a fly ball against the outfield fence. The injury forced him to miss most of the second half of the season.

It was a terrible blow to Williams, who at the age of 32 was probably on the way to his best season ever. The broken arm sapped him of his strength, and even after he returned to action his true power never fully returned. Still, he ended the year with 28 home runs and 97 RBIs in only 89 games played, a remarkable achievement.

There were bright moments, too. Before the start of the 1950 campaign, Williams signed a contract for $100,000, making him the first player ever to reach six figures in a single-season contract.

At the same time, there was no letup in his war with the press. In May 1950, after letting a ground ball get through his legs in left field and hearing boos and catcalls for his error, Williams exploded. Before his next turn at bat, he spit in the direction of the fans. Tom Yawkey, the Red Sox owner, forced the star to apologize publicly for his lack of manners. Grudgingly, Williams did so, and it was front page news all over New England.

The following spring, Williams got off to another poor start with the Boston press. As the Red Sox prepared for the season opener, he felt that his elbow was a bit weak from the previous year. He went to Steve O'Neill, the manager, and asked to be excused from playing in the exhibition games. When word of the request reached the sportswriters, they saw it as one more of Williams's self-centered moves. O'Neill, sensing the same pressure from the press, decided to force Williams to play in most of the spring training games.

As the 1951 season got underway, it was clear to most observers that Williams was not swinging the bat with his old power and authority. He wound up having one of his least impressive years, hitting .318 with 30 home runs and 126 runs batted in. For anyone else, that would have been a wonderful accomplishment. But for Ted Williams, much more was expected.

7

AT WAR AGAIN

In 1952, the United States was at war again, this time in Korea. And once more, able-bodied young men were being drafted to serve in the armed forces. Almost all major leaguers who had served in World War II were left alone when the draft notices went out.

The baseball world was thus stunned when Ted Williams received his draft notice. He was 34 years old, almost twice the age of most draftees. Not only was he disappointed about being recalled to fight; now that he was nearing the age when most ballplayers retired, he wondered if he would ever have a chance to play big league ball again.

Williams went to Korea as a fighter pilot and saw considerable combat action. On one flight, his jet was hit by enemy fire, and he was forced to crash-land his plane while it was already ablaze. Although shaken up, he was not seriously injured.

As Williams recovered from this incident, he contracted a bad case of pneumonia. The illness

Back in the saddle: Recalled into the U.S. military in 1952, Williams went to Korea and served in the navy as a fighter pilot.

eventually led to his being sent home. But by the time of his discharge, the 1952 season had come and gone, and it was already June 1953. The question was, Could Williams, now almost 35 years old, whip himself back into playing shape?

He gave a quick answer. Back in the Boston Red Sox lineup by late summer, he resumed his old ways, hitting a home run on August 9 in his very first at-bat at Fenway Park. He finished his short season in grand style, banging out a .407 batting average along with 13 home runs.

In the spring of 1954, Williams caught the baseball world by surprise when he declared that the upcoming season would be his last. Perhaps he was spurred to make this announcement when, on the very first day of spring training, he fractured his collarbone while diving to make a catch in the outfield. The injury put him on the shelf right through spring training and into the regular season.

But Williams made it back into the lineup in mid-May and picked up right where he had left off the previous season. After going hitless in his first game back, he put on a spectacular show of batting prowess, collecting eight hits in nine at-bats, including two home runs.

Playing on a weak Red Sox club, Williams went on to have yet another great year, hitting .345 with 28 homers and 89 RBIs in only 117 games. Despite having outhit the league's leading batter, Cleveland Indians second baseman Bobby Avila, by four percentage points, Williams was deprived of the American League batting crown. The rules in those days stated that the hitting champ had to have 400 official at-bats during the season to qualify. The number of Williams's official at-bats stood at 386.

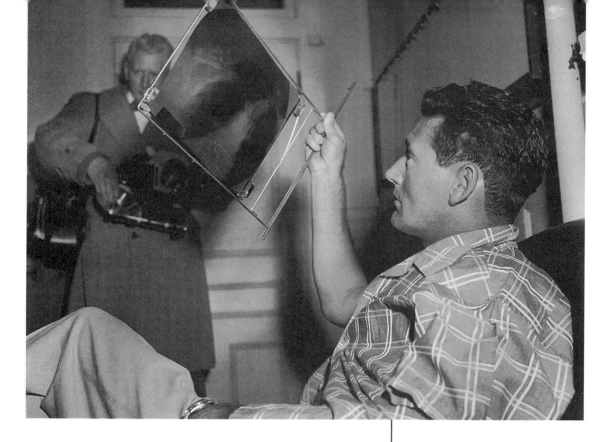

Williams looks at the X ray of his broken left collarbone, which he fractured while diving for a ball on the opening day of spring training in 1954.

Williams had fallen 14 at-bats shy of the necessary 400 in part because he had missed all of April and half of May due to the broken collarbone. But he also did not get enough official at-bats because he frequently received walks. Williams pointed out that he had been walked 136 times during the season, and none of the bases on balls counted as official at-bats.

Years later, the official statistical rules to qualify for a batting crown were changed. Today, all a player needs to qualify for the batting title are 477 plate appearances, a category that includes hits, walks, outs, and sacrifice flies and bunts. Unfortunately for Williams, the rule did not reverse past outcomes, and Avila kept his batting title.

"Gone fishing" was the sign that Ted Williams hung on his door when the spring

This sequence of photographs taken on August 7, 1956, shows Williams spitting at the Boston Red Sox fans in reaction to their alternately booing and cheering him. He was promptly fined $5,000 by the ballclub for "misconduct on the field."

training season of 1955 rolled around. It seemed to all that he had made good on his desire to retire from the game. Yet the baseball bug was still with him, and by May he was back in uniform, slugging line drives all over the American League.

While the Red Sox as a team did poorly, Williams kept up his amazing hitting performances. He completed the 1955 campaign with an average of .356, along with 28 homers and 83 runs batted in. As in the previous year, he had a higher batting average than the eventual American League champ, Detroit Tigers outfielder Al Kaline; but as had happened in the 1954 season, Williams did not qualify for the title because he did not have 400 official at-bats. This time, he had 320 at-bats.

In 1956, Williams batted .345 and clubbed 24 homers. But the season would be remembered more for the time when his war with the press and the fans reached its height. On July 18 in Fenway Park, he hit his 400th career home run. As he crossed the plate, he turned what

should have been a moment of gold to one of
lead by spitting toward the press box. Three
nights later, on the occasion of Joe Cronin Night
at Fenway Park, he did it again.

There was worse coming. On August 7, in the
top of the 11th inning of a scoreless game
against the New York Yankees, Williams dropped
a routine fly ball hit by Mickey Mantle. As the
Yankees center fielder cruised into second base,
the Fenway crowd booed Williams. The next batter, Yogi Berra, slammed a hard fly to left center.
Williams ended the inning by making a fine
catch against the scoreboard. Now the crowd
cheered.

Hearing boos, then cheers, the Red Sox star
snapped. As he raced in from the outfield, he
stopped at the top of the dugout steps and began
spitting at the crowd. Then he turned and spit in
the direction of the press box.

Tom Yawkey had enough of these tantrums
and fined Williams $5,000. It did little good. His
star was not ready to apologize. "I know I'm not
right spitting, but gee, it's the only thing I can
think of doing," he said later. His problem, he
explained, was with the writers who would not
give him a break, and "ten percent" of the fans,
"the baboon type, who's always got his lungs
ready to explode."

But the war went no further. Bit by bit, the
fans began to side with Williams. They started to
cheer him more and more. And the more they
cheered him at each game, the more he felt
appreciated. And the better he did on the field,
the louder the cheers became. It eventually got
to a point where before one game late in the season, he came to the plate and received a stand-
ing ovation from a packed Fenway Park.

Williams, at age 40, stands safely on second after collecting a base hit that assured him of capturing the 1958 American League batting championship. It marked the sixth time he had won the title.

Perhaps buoyed by this fan appreciation, Williams went on to have truly remarkable years in 1957 and 1958. In both seasons, he led the American League in hitting. In 1957, he blistered the ball at an extraordinary .388 clip, missing the .400 mark by only a half dozen hits. He also clobbered 38 home runs along the way. Williams performed these heroics at the age of 39, making him the oldest player ever to win a batting crown. He also led the league in slugging percentage for the ninth time.

During the 1957 season, Williams began to experiment by hitting the ball to left field, something he had never shown any interest in doing in his earlier years. Many opposing ballclubs still used variations of the Boudreau Shift against him, and it was not until this season that he started to slap the pitch the opposite way, toward the Green Monster—the 50-foot-high left-field wall—in Fenway Park.

The following season, 1958, Williams did it again. Now 40 years old, he captured the American League batting championship by hitting .328. But it was not easy. Boston teammate Pete Runnels contended with him all season for the batting crown.

With two games left in the season, both Red Sox hitters were tied at exactly .322. Williams finished with a flurry, gathering five hits in eight at-bats, winding up at .328 to Runnels's .322. With that, Williams won his sixth batting title.

8

"THE GREATEST HITTER WHO EVER LIVED"

Ted Williams had great expectations for the 1959 season. He already had 482 homers under his belt, and he was coming off back-to-back great years with the Boston Red Sox. Hitting 18 more homers was certainly within reason, and that would place him in exclusive company. At the time, only three players—Babe Ruth, Jimmie Foxx, and Mel Ott—had slugged as many as 500 home runs.

During spring training, Williams was practicing his batting stroke when he suddenly felt a sharp twinge in his neck. It was diagnosed as a pinched nerve, serious enough for him to spend two weeks in a hospital recuperating.

Eager to get back into action, Williams returned to the Red Sox lineup but was never really himself at the plate. His neck hurt, and it hurt all year. It showed. He had his worst year in the majors, hitting a career-low .254 with only 10 home runs. He did so poorly that at times he was sent to the bench by the Boston manager.

Had time finally caught up with the great slugger? Now 41 years old, Williams began to

In 1960, his final year in the big leagues, Williams became only the third player in baseball history to hit as many as 500 home runs.

Williams, having taken over as manager of the Washington Senators, confers with coach Nellie Fox (left) at spring training in 1969.

hear the whispers. He continued to claim that his age had nothing to do with his performance, that it was merely the pinched nerve that caused his slump. Regardless, the rumors persisted that perhaps the great Ted Williams should call it quits.

After the season, Tom Yawkey asked Williams about the possibility of retiring. He flat out refused to do so. And, just to show how serious he was about returning to the lineup in 1960, he said to his old friend and boss, "Look, Tom, I'll tell you what. You are currently paying me $125,000 a year to play for you. I'll take a pay cut of $35,000—a 30 percent cut—if you'll let me come back next spring and have one more shot at it."

Yawkey was so stunned by the gesture that he could not help but grant his famous slugger's request. When spring training in 1960 got going, the 41-year-old Williams was raring to start his fourth decade as a major leaguer.

His neck injury fully healed, Williams smacked a tremendous homer in the first game of the regular season. That gave him a total of 493 for his career, tying him with Lou Gehrig. But Williams did not stay tied long. The next day, he hit another.

All told, 1960 was another grand year. Williams hit at a .316 clip, smacked 29 homers, and drove in 72 runs. And on June 17 in Cleveland, he hit career homer number 500 off Wynne Hawkins. Williams blasted 21 more that year, and so he finished with a lifetime total of 521.

But of all the homers that Williams hit in his career, it was the very last one that people remember the most. It happened in the last game he ever played at Fenway Park, in front of a sparse crowd of 10,000 loyal supporters.

It was already known that 1960 would be Williams's last season—he had announced his retirement earlier in the year—and the game against the Baltimore Orioles on September 26 was to be his last performance at Fenway. During the pregame festivities, he thanked his fans for their years of support. But he had less kindly words for the Boston sportswriters, referring to them as the "knights of the keyboard."

When it came to his final at-bat at Fenway, late in the game, Williams ended his career in the most dramatic fashion possible, by belting a home run.

Williams stepped aside from baseball after that season, and when in 1966 he became eligible for induction into the Baseball Hall of Fame,

Nearly a half century after they battled each other for the American League's 1941 Most Valuable Player Award, Ted Williams and Joe DiMaggio sign autographs.

his lifelong dream came true. Not only was he inducted into the Hall of Fame by the nation's sportswriters, but they elected him to baseball's highest honor on the very first ballot.

The years 1960 through 1969 saw Williams pursue his passion for fishing: he went all over the world chasing new fishing spots. By and large, he stayed away from baseball, until 1969, when he returned to the game as the manager of the Washington Senators. In the next three years, the best the Senators could do was a fourth-place finish. The franchise was then moved to Texas and became the Rangers, but that did not change the roster. In the team's first year in Texas, it finished sixth. Williams enjoyed some success in helping his players raise their batting averages. But the ballclub did not have enough talent to fare very well in the American League. After 1972, Williams retired from managing and went back to fishing.

Since then, Williams's main connection with baseball is that he attends the Hall of Fame induction ceremonies each summer at Cooperstown, New York. Meanwhile, the legend of his batting feats continue to grow. And often when he walks down the street, people point to him and say, "There goes the greatest hitter who ever lived."

CHRONOLOGY

1918	Born Theodore Samuel Williams in San Diego, California, on August 30
1936	Signs a contract with the Boston Red Sox; begins playing for the San Diego Padres farm team
1938	Promoted to Boston's top minor league team, the Minneapolis Millers of the International League; finishes the season leading the league in hitting, home runs, and runs batted in
1939	Makes his major league debut with the Boston Red Sox; sets a record for the most runs batted in (145) by a rookie
1941	Hits a three-run homer to carry the American League to victory in the All-Star Game; posts a .735 slugging percentage, hits .406 for the season, and leads the league in home runs (37) and runs batted in (120)
1942	Wins the American League's Triple Crown; joins the U.S. Navy
1943–45	Stationed in Pensacola, Florida, as a flight instructor
1946	Returns to baseball and leads Boston to the American League pennant
1947	Wins his second Triple Crown
1949	Wins his fourth RBI title (159) and home run (43) championship; leads the American league in walks for the sixth straight year
1957	Becomes the oldest player to win a batting crown
1958	Wins his sixth American League batting championship, hitting .328
1960	Hits a home run in the last at-bat of his career at Fenway Park, on September 26
1966	Inducted into the Baseball Hall of Fame
1969	Becomes manager of the Washington Senators
1972	Resigns as Senators manager

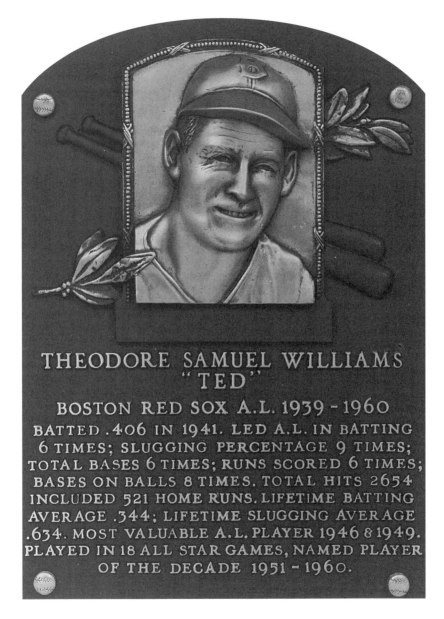

THEODORE SAMUEL WILLIAMS
"TED"

BOSTON RED SOX A.L. 1939-1960
BATTED .406 IN 1941. LED A.L. IN BATTING
6 TIMES; SLUGGING PERCENTAGE 9 TIMES;
TOTAL BASES 6 TIMES; RUNS SCORED 6 TIMES;
BASES ON BALLS 8 TIMES. TOTAL HITS 2654
INCLUDED 521 HOME RUNS. LIFETIME BATTING
AVERAGE .344; LIFETIME SLUGGING AVERAGE
.634. MOST VALUABLE A.L. PLAYER 1946 & 1949.
PLAYED IN 18 ALL STAR GAMES, NAMED PLAYER
OF THE DECADE 1951-1960.

Major League Statistics

Boston Red Sox

YEAR	TEAM	G	AB	R	H	2B	3B	HR	RBI	BA	SB
1939	BOS A	149	565	131	185	44	11	31	145	.327	2
1940		144	561	134	193	43	14	23	113	.344	4
1941		143	456	135	185	33	3	37	120	.406	2
1942		150	522	141	186	34	5	36	137	.356	3
1946		150	514	142	176	37	8	38	123	.342	0
1947		156	528	125	181	40	9	32	114	.343	0
1948		137	509	124	188	44	3	25	127	.369	4
1949		155	566	150	194	39	3	43	159	.343	1
1950		89	334	82	106	24	1	28	97	.317	3
1951		148	531	109	169	28	4	30	126	.318	1
1952		6	10	2	4	0	1	1	3	.400	0
1953		37	91	17	37	6	0	13	34	.407	0
1954		117	386	93	133	23	1	29	89	.345	0
1955		98	320	77	114	21	3	28	83	.356	2
1956		136	400	71	138	28	2	24	82	.345	0
1957		132	420	96	163	28	1	38	87	.388	0
1958		129	411	81	135	23	2	26	85	.328	1
1959		103	272	32	69	15	0	10	43	.254	0
1960		113	310	56	98	15	0	29	72	.316	1
Totals		2292	7706	1798	2654	525	71	521	1839	.344	24

FURTHER READING

Baldassaro, Lawrence, ed. *The Ted Williams Reader.* New York: Simon & Schuster, 1991.

Finlayson, Ann. *Champions at Bat.* Champaign, IL: Garrard, 1974.

Halberstam, David. *The Summer of '49.* New York: Morrow, 1989.

Johnson, Dick, and Glenn Stout. *Ted Williams: A Portrait in Words and Pictures.* Houston: Walker, 1992.

Pope, Edwin. *Ted Williams: The Golden Year.* Englewood Cliffs, NJ: Prentice Hall, 1970.

Seidel, Michael. *Ted Williams: A Baseball Life.* Chicago: Contemporary Books, 1991.

Williams, Ted, and John Underwood. *The Science of Hitting.* New York: Simon & Schuster, 1971.

Williams, Ted, with John Underwood. *My Turn at Bat: The Story of My Life.* New York: Simon & Schuster, 1969.

INDEX

All-Star Game, 28, 33, 42
American League, 10, 11, 25, 27, 28, 39, 48, 56, 57
Avila, Bobby, 46, 47
Baltimore Orioles, 55
Baseball Hall of Fame, 55–56, 57
Berra, Yogi, 49
Boston, Massachusetts, 27
Boston Red Sox, 9, 10, 17, 19, 20, 21, 23, 25, 36, 37, 39, 42, 46, 48, 49, 51, 53
    win 1946 American League pennant, 33, 36
Boudreau, Lou, 34, 35, 36
Boudreau Shift, 34–36, 39, 50
Brooklyn Dodgers, 36
Cannon, Jimmy, 28
Chapman, Ben, 21, 23
Chicago White Sox, 27
Cincinnati, Ohio, 28
Cleveland Indians, 23, 34, 36, 40, 46
Cobb, Ty, 9, 21
Cooperstown, New York, 57
Cramer, Doc, 21
Cronin, Joe, 10, 32, 49
Detroit Tigers, 9, 10, 41, 48
DiMaggio, Joe, 28, 40
Essick, Bill, 16–17
Fenway Park, 24, 25, 32, 33, 39, 46, 48, 49, 50, 55
Fowler, Dick, 10, 11, 12
Foxx, Jimmie, 25, 53
Gehrig, Lou, 24, 55
Haffner, Mickey, 36
Hawkins, Wynne, 55
Heilmann, Harry, 9
Herbert Hoover High School, 16, 17
Hornsby, Rogers, 9, 21
International League, 20, 21

Jackson, Shoeless Joe, 9
Jimmy Fund, 39
Kaline, Al, 48
Kell, George, 41
Korea, 45
Lincoln, Abraham, 27
Mack, Connie, 11, 12
Mantle, Mickey, 49
Minneapolis, Minnesota, 21
Minneapolis Millers, 20
Navy aviation program, 32
New York Yankees, 9, 16, 23, 27, 40, 49
O'Neill, Steve, 43
Orlando, Johnny, 9, 10, 39
Ott, Mel, 53
Pacific Coast League, 19
Parnell, Mel, 40
Pearl Harbor, Hawaii, 31
Pensacola, Florida, 32
Philadelphia, Pennsylvania, 9
Philadelphia Athletics, 9, 10, 11, 12
Pippen, Cotton, 19, 24
Roosevelt, Franklin D., 31
Runnels, Pete, 51
Ruth, Babe, 23, 53
St. Louis Cardinals, 16, 21, 36, 37
San Diego, California, 16, 17, 19, 21
San Diego Padres, 19
Sarasota, Florida, 19
Sewell, Rip, 33
Shibe Park, 9
Terry, Bill, 10
Texas Rangers, 56
Updike, John, 24
Vosmik, Joe, 21
Washington, George, 28
Washington Senators, 56
Webb, Mel, 40

Williams, Barbara Joyce (daughter), 21
Williams, Claudia (daughter), 21
Williams, Danny (brother), 15
Williams, Dolores Wettach (third wife), 21
Williams, Doris Soule (first wife), 21
Williams, John Henry (son), 15
Williams, Lee Howard (second wife), 21
Williams, May (mother), 15, 16–17, 31
Williams, Sam (father), 15, 31
Williams, Theodore Samuel
    All-Star Game appearances, 28, 29, 33, 42
    bats .400, 9–13, 50
    batting championships, 41, 46, 50, 51
    birth, 15
    and Boston sportswriters, 20, 24, 25, 26, 39–40, 43, 48, 49, 55
    childhood in San Diego, 15–17
    feuding with fans, 43, 49
    and fishing, 32, 47, 56, 57
    400th career home run, 48–49
    500th career home run, 53, 55
    Hall of Fame induction, 56
    last at-bat, 55
    major league career, 23–29, 32–43, 46–55
    military service, 31–33, 45–46
    minor league career, 19–21
    Most Valuable Player Award, 28, 40
    $100,000 salary, 42–43
    retirement, 48, 54, 55
    superior eyesight, 12, 32, 33
    wins Triple Crown, 32, 39, 40, 41
World Series, 36–37, 40, 42
World War II, 33, 45
Yankee Stadium, 40
Yawkey, Tom, 49, 54

PICTURE CREDITS
AP/Wide World Photos: pp. 2, 20, 24, 30, 47, 54, 58; AP/Wide World Photos, print courtesy National Baseball Library, Cooperstown, NY: p. 42; National Baseball Library, Cooperstown, NY: pp. 22, 33, 34–35, 40, 44, 60; San Diego Historical Society, Union Tribune Collection: p. 18; *The Sporting News*: pp. 14, 16, 32, 38; UPI/Bettmann: pp. 11, 26, 41, 48, 50, 52, 56; UPI/Bettmann, print courtesy Cleveland Public Library: p. 8

RICK WOLFF is the editorial director of sports books for Macmillan in New York City. A former professional player in the Detroit Tigers' minor league organization, Wolff has written several books about baseball, including *The Psychology of Winning Baseball* (Parker, 1986), *Breaking Into the Big Leagues* (Leisure, 1988), and *Baseball: A Laughing Matter* (*The Sporting News*, 1987). He also does on-air baseball analysis for ESPN, SportsChannel, and the Madison Square Garden Network.

JIM MURRAY, veteran sports columnist of the *Los Angeles Times*, is one of America's most acclaimed writers. He has been named "America's Best Sportswriter" by the National Association of Sportscasters and Sportswriters 14 times, was awarded the Red Smith Award, and was twice winner of the National Headliner Award. In addition, he was awarded the J. G. Taylor Spink Award in 1987 for "meritorious contributions to baseball writing." With this award came his 1988 induction into the National Baseball Hall of Fame in Cooperstown, New York. In 1990, Jim Murray was awarded the Pulitzer Prize for Commentary.

EARL WEAVER is the winningest manager in Baltimore Orioles history by a wide margin. He compiled 1,480 victories in his 17 years at the helm. After managing eight different minor league teams, he was given the chance to lead the Orioles in 1968. Under his leadership the Orioles finished lower than second place in the American League East only four times in 17 years. One of only 12 managers in big league history to have managed in four or more World Series, Earl was named Manager of the Year in 1979. The popular Weaver had his number 5 retired in 1982, joining Brooks Robinson, Frank Robinson, and Jim Palmer, whose numbers were retired previously. Earl Weaver continues his association with the professional baseball scene by writing, broadcasting, and coaching.